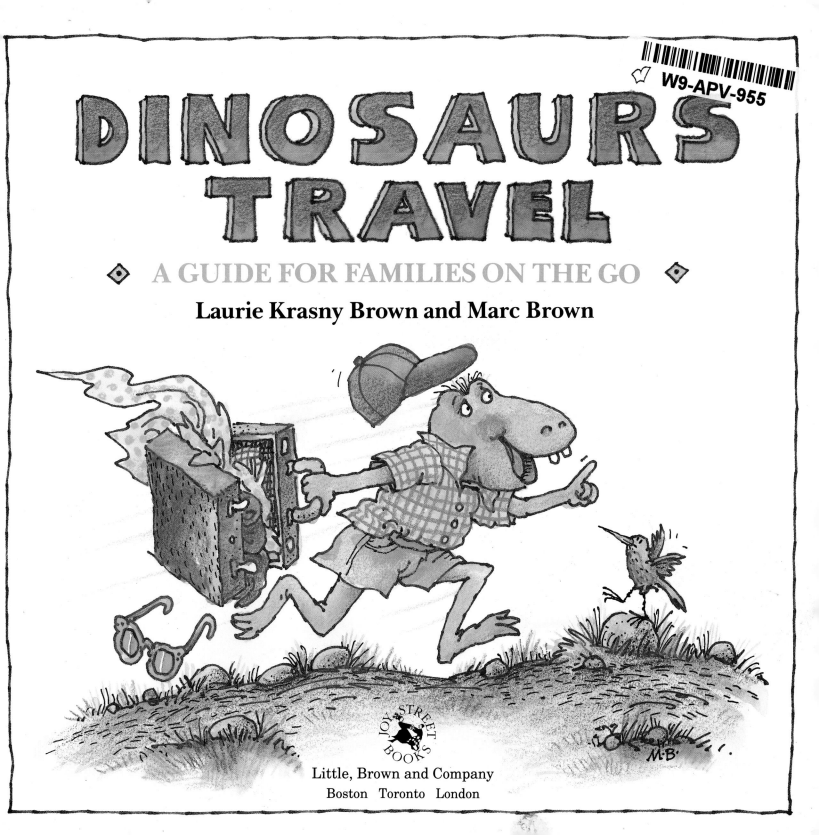

DINOSAURS TRAVEL

A GUIDE FOR FAMILIES ON THE GO

Laurie Krasny Brown and Marc Brown

Little, Brown and Company
Boston Toronto London

◈ FOR PAT AND NOEL ◈

TWO TERRIFIC TRAVEL AGENTS

First Edition

Library of Congress Cataloging-in-Publication Data

Brown, Laurene Krasny.
    Dinosaurs travel.
        p.   cm.
    Summary: Text and illustrations of dinosaur characters discuss
the practicalities and pleasures of travel, from packing up and taking
off to returning home again.
    ISBN 0-316-11076-0 (hc)
    ISBN 0-316-11253-4 (pb)
    1. Travel — Juvenile literature. [1. Travel] I. Brown, Marc Tolon.
II. Title.
G151.B765 1988   87-36637

Joy Street Books are published by Little, Brown and Company (Inc.)

HC: 10 9 8 7 6 5 4 3 2 1
PB: 10 9 8 7 6 5 4 3 2 1

WOR

Published simultaneously in Canada
by Little, Brown & Company (Canada) Limited

Printed in the United States of America

Contents

Traveling

Do you ever wish you could climb a mountain,

fly through the air,

or ride around town in a long limousine?

Every time you leave home, whether to travel

around the world,

or around the block,
get ready for an adventure!

5

Getting Ready for a Trip

Books and maps can help you learn about a new place before you go there.

You may not be able to take your pets with you, but someone else will take good care of them.

If you take the addresses of friends and relatives, you can write to them while you're away.

Find out about the weather where you're going and choose clothes that will be good to wear.

Only pack a few toys, games, books, and tapes.   Small, light, and sturdy things travel best.

Remember one or two favorite companions.

And don't forget these!

Getting From Place to Place

On Foot

Walking lets you stop and see the sights.

You may meet other travelers along the way.

You can hike on a trail where almost no one ever goes.

And your body is all that you need!

Your Own Wheels

Bicycles and skateboards are faster than walking.

You're the driver! It's up to you to know the rules of the road.

Keep your bike or board in good working order, so you're all set to ride anytime.

With your own set of wheels, you can go most anywhere!

You and your family can go biking together.

Sometimes you have to pedal hard to get where you're going,

but downhill you get a free ride!

11

By Car

Cars will take you on all kinds of roads. Riding on the highways is fastest!

Driving on back roads is slower but you see more.

You and your family can go wherever or whenever you want.

You can bring along lots of your things—if you have room!

You and your family can play word games while you ride. You can take turns reading road signs or looking at different license plates.

It feels good to get out and stretch your legs from time to time.

Switching seats will give you different views.

If you have a cassette player, you can bring your favorite tapes.

13

Riding the Subway and Bus

In some cities riding underground in a subway is the fastest way to travel.

On a bus you can see what's going on outside. A tour bus driver will point out the sights.

On a subway or bus you must pay a fare to ride.

Subways and buses make many stops. Don't forget to watch for yours!

Taking the Train

You can buy a ticket for the train at the station. Look at the signs for your track and departure time.

All aboard!

Taking the train is a great way to see new places!

On most trains, you can sit facing forward or backward.

The conductor announces each stop the train makes. You can follow along with a timetable.

Trains don't have to stop until they pull into a station.

The train stops at many stations so passengers can get on and off.

By Boat

Boats can take you across an ocean,

S.S. TRICERATOPS

down rapids,

or to an island in the middle of a lake.

Some ferryboats carry cars and trucks as well as passengers.

It's smart to wear a life jacket in a small boat.

To travel on some boats, *you* have to do all the work!

Flying in Planes

At the airport an agent looks at your ticket, checks your luggage, and assigns you a seat on the plane.

Airport security makes sure no one carries anything dangerous or illegal on the plane.

You can bring a small bag on most planes and stow it under or above your seat. Buckle up!

Take off!

As the plane climbs higher, things below look smaller and smaller.

You'll fly up above the clouds!

If taking off makes your ears hurt, keep swallowing, chew gum, or suck on candy. When the "Fasten Seatbelts" sign goes off, you can stretch or move around.

Pay attention to instructions about what to do in an emergency.

Every seat has special buttons and equipment. You can turn on your overhead light to read.

When you land, the plane puts down its wheels and taxis to the gate. You're back on the ground!

Visiting a New Place

No matter where you travel, it will be different from home.

When you explore a new place, you might be surprised at what you find.

PALACE MOTEL WITH POOL

We can swim at the beach.

POOL CLOSED

Here's your chance to try all kinds of new things!

Eating Away From Home

Some trains have a snack car

or a dining car where you sit down and eat a meal.

On some planes flight attendants serve meals and drinks.

Some boats have a galley for cooking.

When you're in a new place, you can picnic outdoors,

or go to a fancy restaurant.

Hotels may serve meals right in your room.

Don't be afraid to taste new foods!

25

Sleeping Away From Home

On some vehicles you can sleep while you travel and wake up somewhere else.

Boats may have cabins for sleeping.

On long plane flights you can push your seat back and sleep. You may wake up thousands of miles away!

Some trains have sleeping cars.

You can pitch a tent in a special spot and crawl into a sleeping bag.

In a hammock you sleep under the stars.

If you stay with relatives, you may share a place to sleep.

In a hotel room, you may have a bed to yourself. Best of all, someone else makes it for you!

27

Traveling Alone

When you travel alone, carry a piece of paper with your name, address, phone number, where you're going, and how you're getting there.

In case of emergency please notify:
Dad- 212-555-184
Mom- 814-838-371
Grammy 203 712-172
Uncle Ed 814-516-
Dawn 617-749-210
Tolon 403-773-137

Keep tickets, important papers, and money safe in a secret hiding place.

Bring along cash and coins for emergencies.

TELEPHONE

ADVENTURE ESCAPE

A flight attendant will let you board early and will help you find a seat.

You may meet other travelers along the way.

Never go off with a stranger.

You may feel more grown up traveling alone—and you are!

Coming Home

When it's time to go home, remember to pack all your things.

You may want to bring back a gift for someone special.

Souvenirs and pictures will remind you of your trip.

GENUINE FOSSIL BONE

At home, things may look different to you.

30

It's fun to go home again and see friends and relatives.

You can play with all your toys,

eat your favorite snacks,

and dream about where to travel next!